Webb

by Iain Gray

Lang**Syne**

PUBLISHING

WRITING *to* REMEMBER

WRITING *to* REMEMBER

79 Main Street, Newtongrange,
Midlothian EH22 4NA
Tel: 0131 344 0414   Fax: 0845 075 6085
E-mail: info@lang-syne.co.uk
www.langsyneshop.co.uk

Design by Dorothy Meikle
Printed by Martins the Printers, Berwick-upon-Tweed
© Lang Syne Publishers Ltd 2013

ISBN 978-1-85217-529-0

Webb

MOTTO:
Be firm.

CREST:
An eagle rising from a crown.

NAME variations include:
Webbe.

Chapter one:

The origins of popular surnames

by George Forbes and Iain Gray

If you don't know where you came from, you won't know where you're going is a frequently quoted observation and one that has a particular resonance today when there has been a marked upsurge in interest in genealogy, with increasing numbers of people curious to trace their family roots.

Main sources for genealogical research include census returns and official records of births, marriages and deaths – and the key to unlocking the detail they contain is obviously a family surname, one that has been 'inherited' and passed from generation to generation.

No matter our station in life, we all have a surname – but it was not until about the middle of the fourteenth century that the practice of being identified by a particular surname became commonly established throughout the British Isles.

Previous to this, it was normal for a person to be identified through the use of only a forename.

But as population gradually increased and there were many more people with the same forename, surnames were adopted to distinguish one person, or community, from another.

Many common English surnames are patronymic in origin, meaning they stem from the forename of one's father – with 'Johnson,' for example, indicating 'son of John.'

It was the Normans, in the wake of their eleventh century conquest of Anglo-Saxon England, a pivotal moment in the nation's history, who first brought surnames into usage – although it was a gradual process.

For the Normans, these were names initially based on the title of their estates, local villages and chateaux in France to distinguish and identify these andholdings.

Such grand descriptions also helped enhance the prestige of these warlords and generally glorify their lofty positions high above the humble serfs slaving away below in the pecking order who had only single names, often with Biblical connotations as in Pierre and Jacques.

The only descriptive distinctions among the peasantry concerned their occupations, like 'Pierre the swineherd' or 'Jacques the ferryman.'

Roots of surnames that came into usage in England not only included Norman-French, but also Old French, Old Norse, Old English, Middle English, German, Latin, Greek, Hebrew and the Gaelic languages of the Celts.

The Normans themselves were originally Vikings, or 'Northmen', who raided, colonised and eventually settled down around the French coastline.

The had sailed up the Seine in their longboats in 900AD under their ferocious leader Rollo and ruled the roost in north eastern France before sailing over to conquer England in 1066 under Duke William of Normandy – better known to posterity as William the Conqueror, or King William I of England.

Granted lands in the newly-conquered England, some of their descendants later acquired territories in Wales, Scotland and Ireland – taking not only their own surnames, but also the practice of adopting a surname, with them.

But it was in England where Norman rule and custom first impacted, particularly in relation to the adoption of surnames.

This is reflected in the famous *Domesday Book*, a massive survey of much of England and Wales, ordered by William I, to determine who owned what, what it was worth and therefore how much they were liable to pay in taxes to the voracious Royal Exchequer.

Completed in 1086 and now held in the National Archives in Kew, London, 'Domesday' was an Old English word meaning 'Day of Judgement.'

This was because, in the words of one contemporary chronicler, "its decisions, like those of the Last Judgement, are unalterable."

It had been a requirement of all those English landholders – from the richest to the poorest – that they identify themselves for the purposes of the survey and for future reference by means of a surname.

This is why the *Domesday Book*, although written in Latin as was the practice for several centuries with both civic and ecclesiastical records, is an invaluable source for the early appearance of a wide range of English surnames.

Several of these names were coined in connection with occupations.

These include Baker and Smith, while Cooks, Chamberlains, Constables and Porters were to be found carrying out duties in large medieval households.

The church's influence can be found in names such as Bishop, Friar and Monk while the popular name of Bennett derives from the late fifth to mid-sixth century Saint Benedict, founder of the Benedictine order of monks.

The early medical profession is represented by Barber, while businessmen produced names that include Merchant and Sellers.

Down at the village watermill, the names that cropped up included Millar/Miller, Walker and Fuller while other self-explanatory trades included Cooper, Tailor, Mason and Wright.

Even the scenery was utilised as in Moor, Hill, Wood and Forrest – while the hunt and the chase supplied names that include Hunter, Falconer, Fowler and Fox.

Colours are also a source of popular surnames as in Black, Brown, Gray/Grey, Green and White, and would have denoted the colour of the clothing the person habitually wore or, apart from the obvious exception of 'Green', one's hair colouring or even complexion.

The surname Red developed into Reid, whil

Blue was rare and no-one wanted to be associated with yellow.

Rather self-important individuals took surnames that include Goodman and Wiseman, while physical attributes crept into surnames such as Small and Little.

Many families proudly boast the heraldic device known as a Coat of Arms, as featured on our front cover.

The central motif of the Coat of Arms would originally have been what was borne on the shield of a warrior to distinguish himself from others on the battlefield.

Not featured on the Coat of Arms, but highlighted on page three, is the family motto and related crest – with the latter frequently different from the central motif.

Adding further variety to the rich cultural heritage that is represented by surnames is the appearance in recent times in lists of the 100 most common names found in England of ones that include Khan, Patel and Singh – names that have proud roots in the vast sub-continent of India.

Echoes of a far distant past can still be found in our surnames and they can be borne with pride in commemoration of our forebears.

Chapter two:

Ancient roots

An occupational surname that has been present in the British Isles from the earliest times, 'Webb' derives from the Old English 'web' or 'webbe', meaning a woven cloth or to weave – and originally denoted someone who worked as a weaver.

In common with many other popular English surnames of today, it became particularly common-place in the wake of the Norman Conquest of 1066 – but it is of much earlier Anglo-Saxon roots.

Flowing through the veins of many people of English birth today is the blood of those Germanic tribes who invaded and settled in the south and east of the island of Britain from about the early fifth century.

Known as the Anglo-Saxons, they were composed of the Jutes, from the area of the Jutland Peninsula in modern Denmark, the Saxons from Lower Saxony, in modern Germany and the Angles from the Angeln area of Germany.

It was the Angles who gave the name 'Engla land', or 'Aengla land' – better known as 'England.'

They held sway in what became known as England from approximately 550 to 1066, with the main kingdoms those of Sussex, Wessex, Northumbria, Mercia, Kent, East Anglia and Essex.

Whoever controlled the most powerful of these kingdoms was tacitly recognised as overall 'king' – one of the most noted being Alfred the Great, King of Wessex from 871 to 899.

It was during his reign that the famous *Anglo-Saxon Chronicle* was compiled – an invaluable source of Anglo-Saxon history – while Alfred was designated in early documents as *Rex Anglorum Saxonum*, King of the English Saxons.

Through the Anglo-Saxons, the language known as Old English developed, later transforming from the eleventh century into Middle English – sources from which many popular English surnames of today, such as Webb, derive.

Following the battle of Hastings in October of 1066, that saw the death of Harold II, last of the Anglo-Saxon kings, William Duke of Normandy was declared King of England on December 25, and the complete subjugation of his Anglo-Saxon subjects followed.

Those Normans who had fought on his

behalf were rewarded with the lands of Anglo-Saxons, many of whom sought exile abroad as mercenaries.

Within an astonishingly short space of time, Norman manners, customs and law were imposed on England – laying the basis for what subsequently became established 'English' custom and practice.

But beneath the surface, old Anglo-Saxon culture was not totally eradicated.

Some aspects were absorbed into those of the Normans, while faint echoes of the Anglo-Saxon past is still seen today in the form of popular surnames such as Webb.

The name first made its appearance in Wiltshire, while an Osbert Webbe is recorded in Suffolk in 1221 and Alice la Webbe in Colchester in 1327.

Bearers of the name figure prominently in Britain's frequently turbulent historical record.

Not only a leading early eighteenth century military figure but also a politician, Lieutenant-General John Webb was born into a distinguished family in the ancient Webb heartland of Wiltshire in 1667.

His father, Colonel Edmund Webb, held a

position in the household of Prince George of Denmark while a second cousin, Henry St John, became Tory leader in Parliament during the reign from 1702 to 1714 of Queen Anne.

Acquiring great wealth through his marriage in 1690 to the daughter of the landowner Henry Borlase, and at the time a Cornet of Dragoons, he bought the estate of Biddesden House, at Ludgershall, in his native Wiltshire.

Promoted a year after his marriage to Colonel of Princess Anne of Denmark's Regiment of Foot, he was also elected as a Tory Member of Parliament (MP).

During the 1702 to 1713 War of the Spanish Succession against France, he fought at the battle of Blenheim, in Bavaria, in August of 1704; promoted to Major-General, he also fought later at the battles of Ramillies and Oudenarde.

He further distinguished himself in September of 1708 when, commanding the British troops at the battle of Wijnendale, he protected a convoy that was delivering vital supplies to the besiegers of Lille.

Further battle honours came in September of 1709 when, by now a Lieutenant-General, he saw action at the battle of Malplaquet.

The bloodiest battle of the War of the Spanish

Succession, a combined army of 100,000 British, Dutch, German and Austrian soldiers met with a 90,000-strong French army who were holding Mons, in Belgium.

Although the allied army eventually forced the surrender of Mons, they lost 24,000 killed or wounded, while the French lost 12,000.

Severely wounded at Malplaquet, Webb was awarded a substantial pension and later appointed Governor of the Isle of Wight.

He died in 1724, while his brother Thomas Webb was an ancestor of the great English writer William Makepeace Thackeray, the author of *Vanity Fair*.

In a later century and on much different battlefields, General Alexander Stewart Webb was the recipient of the Medal of Honor, America's highest award for military valour.

Born in New York City in 1835, he was the son of the newspaper owner and diplomat Alexander Webb, while his grandfather Samuel Bletchley Webb had served on the staff of George Washington during the American War of Independence of 1775 to 1783.

Graduating from the United States Military Academy in 1855, on the outbreak of the Civil War six years later he saw action at the First Battle of Bull Run and served as aide-de-camp to Brigadier General William F. Barry, chief of artillery of the Union's Army of the Potomac.

Responsible for assembling a line of artillery defence during the battle of Malvern Hill in July of 1862, it was said later that he had saved the Union Army from destruction.

It was at the battle of Gettysburg in July of the following year that he performed the actions for which he was awarded the Medal of Honor.

With his brigade posted on Cemetery Ridge, he managed to repulse a fierce assault by Confederate troops and capture about 300 of their number.

He died in 1911, while there is a statue of him at Gettysburg.

Back to British shores, Lieutenant-General Sir Henry Webb commanded the 13th Battalion Gloucestershire Regiment and the 14th Battalion Worcestershire regiment during the First World War.

Also a Liberal Party politician who served as a Junior Lord of the Treasury, he was created a baronet in 1916; born in Hereford in 1866, he died in 1940.

A captain in the 17th Lancers and also a

wealthy landowner, William Webb was born in Sussex in 1829.

It was following the death of his father in 1847 that he inherited estates in Co. Durham, Yorkshire and Lincolnshire.

Before his death in 1899, he bought Newstead Abbey in Ravenshead, Nottingham – outbidding Queen Victoria for the magnificent property.

Chapter three:

Daring spirits

Bearers of the Webb name have distinguished themselves in the field of social reform – no less so that Sidney Webb and his wife Beatrice.

Born in 1859, Sidney and Beatrice, who was born in 1858, were among the founders of the London School of Economics and Political Science – more commonly known today as LSE – while they were also leading intellectual lights of the political 'think-tank' known as the Fabian Society.

A member of the Labour Party, Sidney Webb served as both Secretary of State for the Colonies and Secretary of State for Dominion Affairs under the Labour Government of Ramsay MacDonald.

He co-authored, along with his wife, the 1894 *A History of Trade Unionism*, while the couple also wrote widely on socialism in general and social reform in particular.

Raised to the Peerage of the United Kingdom as 1st Baron Passfield, Sidney Webb died in 1947, four years after his wife; their ashes are interred in the nave of Westminster Abbey.

Bearers of the Webb name have also left enduring legacies on the landscape.

Born in 1611 in Smithfield, London, John Webb was the architect and scholar who, during the early seventeenth century English Civil War acted as a spy for Charles I.

This was in his capacity of deputy surveyor, when he secretly sent the Royalists the plans for what were known as London's Lines of Communication – giving the number and locations of guns that the Parliamentarians had mounted to protect the city.

A son-in-law of fellow architect and theatre designer Inigo Jones, in 1654 he designed the first classical portico on an English country house – at The Vyne, Hampshire.

He died in 1672, while also having been responsible for the design of Gunnersbury House, in Ealing, and King Charles Court, which later formed part of Greenwich Hospital.

Born in 1821 in Sudbury, Suffolk but immigrating to Australia and settling in Victoria, Charles Webb was the architect responsible for major works in Melbourne that include the city's Tasma Terrace, South Melbourne Town Hall and the Windsor Hotel; he died in 1898.

With many noted works that include the re-design of the East Front façade of Buckingham Palace, completed in 1913, and The Mall approach to the palace, Sir Aston Webb was the architect born in London in 1849.

President of the Royal Academy from 1919 to 1924 and the recipient of the Royal Gold Medal for Architecture and the American Institute of Architects Gold Medal, other works include London's Victoria Memorial and Birmingham University; he died in 1930.

Known as the 'Father of Arts and Crafts Architecture', Philip Webb was born in Oxford in 1931.

Particularly noted for his design of the Red House, at Bexleyheath, southeast London, he was also one of the founders of the Society for the Protection of Ancient Buildings; he died in 1915.

Reaching for the heavens, James E. Webb, born in Granville County, North Carolina in 1906, served from 1961 to 1968 as the second administrator of the American space agency NASA; a recipient of the Presidential Medal of Freedom, he died in 1992.

One particularly notorious bearer of the otherwise proud name of Webb was the American Old West gunfighter and outlaw John Webb.

Born in 1847 in Keokuk County, Iowa, by 1871 he was working as a buffalo hunter when he made the acquaintance in Dodge City, Kansas of the legendary Wyatt Earp and Bat Masterson.

Seven years later, when Masterton was appointed sheriff of Ford County, he deputised Webb to help track down outlaws who had robbed a train.

Later settling in Las Vegas, New Mexico he partnered Doc Holliday for a time in running a saloon before being appointed town marshal.

But despite his trusted position as a lawman, Webb turned to a life of crime, becoming a member of the feared Dodge City Gang that, ironically, was led by the colourfully named Hoodoo Brown – a Justice of the Peace.

The gang was responsible for a number of train and stagecoach robberies and murders, and Webb was eventually arrested for murder in April of 1880 and sentenced to hang.

The sentence was later commuted to life imprisonment, but in September of the following year, aided by former gang members, he succeeded in a daring escape from prison.

On the run from the law, he changed his name to Samuel King – but died from smallpox in

Winslow, Arkansas, only a few months after his prison break.

One particularly dare-devil but ultimately unfortunate bearer of the proud name of Webb was Captain Matthew Webb.

Born in 1848 in Dawley, Shropshire, he was the first person to swim the English Channel without the use of artificial aids.

He had already become something of a British national hero before he entered the record books for this feat.

He had joined the Merchant Navy when aged 12 and, a number of years later while serving as a mate aboard the Cunard Line ship *Russia*, sailing from New York to Liverpool, he dived into the freezing waters of the mid-Atlantic to rescue a man who had fallen overboard.

His daring rescue attempt failed, but he was awarded £100 and the prestigious Stanhope Medal of the Royal Humane Society.

Feted by the national press, he hit the headlines again when, while home on leave, he rescued his 12-year-old brother from drowning in the River Severn, near Ironbridge.

Ten years later, by this time serving as captain

aboard the steamship *Emerald*, he resolved to attempt to swim the English Channel after reading of the failed attempt by fellow Englishman J.B. Johnson.

It was not until August 12 of 1875 that he made his first attempt – but poor sea conditions and high winds forced him to abandon the swim.

Undeterred, he made his second and this time successful attempt twelve days later.

Diving from the Admiralty Pier at Dover and, smeared in porpoise oil and backed by three escort boats, he landed on the beach at Calais after a gruelling 21 hours and 45 minutes in the Channel – with the zigzag course he had taken more than 39 miles (64km) long.

Recognised as a true British hero, his picture was put on boxes of Bryant and May matches – a picture that is thought to have provided the inspiration nearly a century later for the character Inspector Clouseau, portrayed by Peter Sellers in the *Pink Panther* series of films.

His final and most daring stunt came on July 24, 1883, when he attempted to swim through the Whirlpool Rapids below the Niagara Falls in New York State.

Jumping into the river's fast flowing waters

from a small boat located near the Niagara Falls Suspension Bridge, he began to swim, but he drowned in the section of the river near the entrance to the treacherous whirlpool.

His body was recovered and interred in Oakwood Cemetery, Niagara Falls.

There is a memorial to the daring Captain Matthew Webb in his home town of Dawley, while the John Betjeman poem *A Shropshire Lad* commemorates his death with the vivid imagery of his ghost swimming back home.

Chapter four:

On the world stage

Bearers of the Webb name have gained acclaim through a diverse range of pursuits, not least in the world of entertainment.

Born to English parents in 1940 in Lucknow, India, Harry Rodger Webb is the veteran singer, musician and performer better known as **Cliff Richard**.

His father worked for a catering company that serviced the Indian railways and, following the granting of Indian independence in 1947, the family moved back to England and settled in Surrey.

Expressing an interest in skiffle music, the future best-selling singer's father bought him a guitar when he was aged 16.

This helped to set him on the road to stardom, releasing the first of his many hit singles, *Move It*, in 1958.

He adopted the surname 'Richard' in recognition of his American music idol Little Richard and 'Cliff', as in 'rock-face', suggesting 'rock.'

With the Shadows as his backing group, he enjoyed enormous success throughout the late 1950s and early 1960s, appearing with the band in films that include *The Young Ones* and *Summer Holiday*.

Parting company with the Shadows, who remained a best-selling band in their own right, he became a devout Christian and, in addition to recording hits that include *The Day I Met Marie*, *Miss You Nights*, *We Don't Talk Anymore* and *Devil Woman*, he also recorded gospel music.

Representing the United Kingdom in the 1968 Eurovision Song Contest with *Congratulations*, he was placed second, while five years later he was placed third with *Power to All Our Friends*.

Having had more than 130 singles, EPs and albums in the UK Top 20 than any other artist and having sold an estimated 250 million records world-wide, his many honours include two Ivor Novello Awards and three Brit Awards that include a Lifetime Achievement Award.

The recipient of both an OBE and a knight-hood, he was ranked at 56th in the 2002 '100 Greatest Britons' list, sponsored by the BBC and voted for by the public.

A life-long bachelor, he has stated, however, that at one time he had considered marriage to the British former tennis star Sue Barker.

Also on British shores, **Marti Webb** is the musical actress who played the role of Evita Peron from 1979 to 1980 in the stage musical *Evita*.

Also starring in Andrew Lloyd Webber's one-woman show *Tell Me on a Sunday*, she enjoyed chart success with *Take That Look Off Your Face*.

Born in 1944 in Cricklewood, London other hit singles include the 1990 *Don't Let the Moment Pass*, while she also starred in the 2008 stage production of *Blood Brothers*.

The only artist to have received Grammy Awards in the separate categories of music, lyrics and orchestration, **Jimmy Webb** is the American song-writer who has written a string of best-selling and memorable hits for a wide range of artists.

These include the 1967 *Up, Up and Away*, by The 5th Dimension, *By the Time I Get to Phoenix* and *Wichita Lineman*, by Glen Campbell, and *MacArthur Park*, by Richard Harris, in addition to songs recorded by other artists who include The Supremes, Frank Sinatra and Elvis Presley.

Born in 1946 in Elk City, Oklahoma, his numerous awards include the 1993 National Academy of Songwriters Lifetime Achievement Award, while he is also the author of the 1998 book *Tunesmith: Inside the Art of Songwriting*.

In contemporary music, **Gary Webb**, born in 1958 in Hammersmith, London is the English singer, musician and composer better known by his stage name of Gary Numan.

Considered a pioneer of commercial electronic music, he enjoyed hits with his band Tubeway Army with the 1979 *Are Friends Electric?* and *Cars*.

Born in 1978 in Moss Side, Manchester, **Simon Webbe** is the English singer, songwriter and actor best known as a member of the band Blue.

First formed as a boy band in 2000, Blue split up in 2005 after enjoying hits that include *Too Close* and *If You Come Back*.

They reformed in 2009 and represented the United Kingdom in the 2011 Eurovision Song Contest in Germany, finishing in eleventh place with *I Can*.

From music to the stage, Webb Parmelee Hollenbeck, born in 1889 in Indianapolis, was the American actor better known by his stage name of **Clifton Webb**.

Known for his Academy Award-nominated roles in films that include the 1944 *Laura*, the 1946 *The Razor's Edge* and, from 1949, *Sitting Pretty*, other screen credits include the 1952 *Stars and Stripes Forever* and the 1961 *Satan Never Sleeps*.

The recipient of a star on the Hollywood Walk of Fame, he died in 1966.

Best known for his role of Sergeant Joe Friday from 1951 to 1959 in the popular American radio and television series *Dragnet*, **Jack Webb** was the actor, screenwriter, director and producer born in 1920 in Santa Monica, California.

With big screen acting credits that include the 1950 *Halls of Montezuma* and director credits that include the 1957 *The D.I.* and the recipient of two stars on the Hollywood Walk of Fame, he died in 1982.

Born in 1956 in Greenwich Village, Manhattan, **Chloe Webb** is the American actress who won a Best Actress award from the National Society of Film Critics for her role in the 1986 *Sid and Nancy*.

Other film credits include the 1987 *The Belly of an Architect*, the 1988 *Twins* and, from 2009, *Repo Chick*.

Born in 1904 in Willesden, Middlesex, Olive Webb was the English character actress better known as **Rita Webb**.

Best known as a 'stooge' for comedian

Benny Hill in his long-running British television series, other small screen credits include *Dixon of Dock Green* and *Till Death Us Do Part*.

With big screen credits that include the 1967 *To Sir, with Love* and the 1969 *The Magic Christian*, she died in 1981.

An English actor of both stage and screen, **Alan Webb** was born in 1906 in Scarborough, Yorkshire.

Appearing in a number of Broadway productions, he was nominated for a Tony Award for Best Performance by a Leading Actor in a Play in 1968 for his role in *I Never Sang for My Father*.

With film credits that include the 1949 *Challenge to Lassie*, the 1965 *King Rat* and, from 1977, *The Duellist*, he died in 1982.

Born in London in 1958, **Danny Webb** is the British stage, television and film actor whose television credits include *Brookside*, *The Bill*, *Silent Witness* and *Sherlock*.

On the big screen, his credits include the 1984 *A Year of the Quiet Sun*, the 1992 *Alien 3* and, from 2008, *Valkyrie*.

Born in 1972 in Boston, Lincolnshire, **Robert Webb** is the comedian, actor and writer who is one half, along with David Mitchell, of the double-act Mitchell and Webb.

Their television show *That Mitchell and Webb Look* won the 2007 BAFTA award for Best Comedy Programme or Series, while Webb's other television credits include *My Family*.

Behind the camera lens, **James R. Webb**, born in 1909 in Denver, Colorado and who died in 1974, was the screenwriter who won an Academy Award in 1963 for *How the West Was Won*.

Other film credits include the 1962 *Cape Fear* and, from 1970, *They Call Me MISTER Tibbs!*

Bearers of the Webb name have also excelled, and continue to excel, in the highly competitive world of sport.

Recognised as one of the top players in the history of women's golf, **Karrie Webb** is the Australian golfer born in 1974 in Ayr, Queensland.

Inducted into the World Golf Hall of Fame in 2005, her many wins include the Ladies Professional Golfers Association (LPGA) Championship in 2001, the U.S. Women's Open in 2000 and 2001 and the Women's British Open in 2002.

On the fields of European football, **David Webb** is the former defender who played for teams that include Leyton Orient, Chelsea and Torquay United.

Born in Stratford, London, in 1946 and having managed Chelsea and, since 2010 assistant manager of Southend United, he is the father of **Daniel Webb**, born in 1983, and who has played for teams that include Southampton, Southend United and Dover Athletic.

Rated by the International Federation of Football History and Statistics as among the top football referees of all time, **Howard Webb** is the English referee born in 1971 in Rotherham, Yorkshire.

A former police sergeant and a FIFA-listed referee since 2005, he has officiated at the UEFA Champions League and the FIFA World Cup.

In contemporary sailing, **Sarah Kathleen Webb**, also known since her marriage in 2009 as Sarah Kathleen Webb Gosling, is the British professional sailor who is the recipient of two Olympic gold medals in the Yngling class – with a Yngling being a sailing boat which is a cross between a keelboat and a planing dinghy.

Winner of the gold medal in the discipline, along with Shirley Robertson and Sarah Ayton – collectively known at the time as 'Three Blondes in a

Boat' – she also won gold, along with Pippa Wilson and Sarah Ayton at the 2008 Olympics in Beijing.

Reaching for the heavens, the **Rev. Thomas Webb** was the British amateur astronomer whose nineteenth century guide to the subject remains an important source of reference to this day.

Born in 1807 and ordained a minister in the Anglican Church in 1829, it was in 1852 that he was assigned to the small parish of Hardwicke, near the English border with Wales.

Observing the heavens by telescope from a small wood and canvas observatory that he built in the grounds of his vicarage, he went on to write his classic two-volume astronomical observing guide *Celestial Objects for Common Telescopes.*

First published in 1859, nearly thirty years before his death in 1885, it contains instructions for amateur astronomers on the use of telescopes and descriptions of what can be observed through them in the skies above.